This Book is
Protected by
Instant IP

WHAT OTHERS ARE SAYING

As a pastor and friend of Laura Johnson, I can attest that her book is a compelling testimony. Laura has walked through the depths of heartache and pain, which would have caused many to lose hope. Yet her testimony speaks volumes not only of the redemptive power of Christ but also of the courage it takes to surrender to Him despite the heartache and pain. Laura is a shining example of one who has learned how to conquer the trials and tribulations that threaten to undo us. Thus, her story is one of hope, compassion, and wisdom that is well beyond her years. It is with great joy and confidence that I can recommend her book to you. Her journey is a testament to the fact that heartache and pain are neither final nor do they have to define you. For in Christ, there is not only hope and healing but also ultimate restoration.

—Charlie Barnes, Pastor

Meeting Laura felt serendipitous. I immediately knew she carried a message that would reach far beyond herself. Her sincerity, strength, and faith are authentic and unmistakable. I Am the Other Woman *reveals Laura taking a painful chapter and allowing God to shape it into something honest and compassionate—something to be used as a healing aid for others. She speaks with a voice full of empathy, courage, spiritual maturity, and transformation. Her story will resonate with anyone longing for redemption, restoration, and hope.*

—Sasha Tripp, Owner of Story House Real Estate

I have known Laura and her family for more than 10 years. She has a sincere heart to help others and a desire to follow God in her daily walk. In this book, Laura shares her insight on how infidelity affects not just the couple involved but everyone around them. She shares her own personal journey to show us how to move forward as one navigates through the emotional complexities surrounding being "the other woman." This book shows a rare and courageous glimpse into the heartbreak of an affair, and how God can use our missteps to bring us back into His will and bless us beyond what we could ever expect. A must-read!

—Cheryl U'Ran

I AM THE OTHER WOMAN

Escape the Pain, Restore the Hope, Become the Person You Were Created to Be

I AM THE OTHER WOMAN

Escape the Pain, Restore the Hope, Become the Person You Were Created to Be

Laura M. Johnson

ethos
collective

DEDICATION

To all who have been touched by the profound consequences of infidelity: your stories, shared with me over the years, have revealed a depth of experience I could never have imagined. Whether you are the other person, the wounded spouse, the one who erred, the children and extended families, or the communities and churches affected, you have inspired these words. Though we strive to move forward and live unburdened by the past, it remains essential to remember that many still carry the weight of these circumstances, often silently and unseen.

This dedication is a gentle reminder to each of you. You are seen, cherished, heard, and supported as you navigate the daily journey of healing from pain, in whatever form it may take. The past decade of my life has been marked by failure, sorrow, and shame, but also by triumph and, ultimately, restoration through the boundless grace of my Saviour, Jesus Christ. This book is offered to those who are ready to escape the pain, restore the hope, and become the person you were created to be.

Blessings to you all,

Laura

TABLE OF CONTENTS

Foreword. 15

How It All Began 17

PART I
Hurt

Chapter One: It Could Never Happen to Me 23

Chapter Two: How Could it Happen Again?. 35

Chapter Three: Choose Your Hard 41

PART II
Hope

Chapter Four: Darkness to Light. 49

Chapter Five: God Sees You 59

Chapter Six: Seen, Heard, and Acknowledged. 67

Chapter Seven: Forgiven, Redeemed, and Restored 75

PART III
Healing

Chapter Eight: For Those Affected by the Fallout 85

Chapter Nine: The Future of the Other Woman 91

Where Do We Go From Here? 97

Endnotes. 99

Acknowledgments. 101

About the Author 103

FOREWORD

Charles Spurgeon, the influential pastor and evangelist, once wrote, "The more you have, the more you are in debt to God." Those words ring true as you open this book, because what you're about to read is a story marked by both deep brokenness and extraordinary grace.

Infidelity. Most people don't want to think about the word, let alone speak it aloud. It carries pain, shame, and memories many would rather keep buried. Yet nearly all of us are touched by it in some way. Maybe it has marked your life, or the life of someone you love. And still, conversations about infidelity remain whispers in the dark—quiet, hidden, spoken only in the shadows where people fear being seen or judged.

Laura and I met more than a decade before she wrote this book, and I have witnessed—and lived through—much of what you will read. This is a story of failure, struggle, redemption, and restoration. In that sense, it mirrors the human experience. Laura is taking a bold and courageous step in sharing her journey so openly. She is shining a light on a topic many avoid, not to sensationalize it, but to help you or someone you care about take steps toward healing, forgiveness, and freedom. When we bring hard things into the light, they lose their power over us.

Laura grew up in a conservative Christian home, the kind where, as she says, "if the church doors were open, we were there." She attended Christian schools and later Bible college. That is the lens through which she writes—a lens shaped by faith, Scripture, and a longing to honor God even in the midst of failure. If your background is different, or if you've had little exposure to church—or even painful experiences with it—I encourage you to read with an open heart. Her story is not about religion; it is about redemption.

True love is always an act of sacrifice. Laura is loving you through these pages by sacrificing the comfort of secrecy. She is giving up the anonymity she lived behind for years so that others might find the courage to face their own stories. She offers her journey not to excuse her past, but to create space for you to confront yours—to know it is okay to talk about what hurts, and to believe that healing is possible.

So yes, Laura is a wife and mom of three and bonus mom of four, a woman who helps run multiple businesses, volunteers in women's ministry, gives generously, and befriends easily. To me, she is a Proverbs 31 Woman, yet to many she will always be labeled "The Other Woman."

But this book is her declaration that a label is not a life sentence. It is her testimony that God writes better endings than we do. And it is her invitation for you to step into the light, too.

Great reading to you,

Mark H. Johnson
CFP®, AEP®, BFA™, CEPA®, CDFA, JD, and MBA,
And more importantly, Laura's husband.

HOW IT ALL BEGAN

"I'll be leaving in a couple of days and will be gone all next week. I have to go, Laura. It's work."

Everything pivoted the night my husband spoke those words.

Nolan and I had been in counseling with the pastor of our church for months. All the things I thought we could work out when we met in college had become major problems. I needed a strong leader and someone who would grow spiritually with me. Even though I knew he was weaker in those areas before we married, I thought, since we were heading into ministry, he would develop those strengths. After all, I had my own growing to do, too. Unfortunately, the entirety of our marriage had been a continuous cycle of defeat.

That night, when he chose his business trip over our marriage, I knew in my heart we were done. Through tears, I had begged him to stay. I knew our marriage was in the darkest moment ever. "Nolan, we need to work on our relationship. Can't someone else in your company go on this trip? Please, just ask."

"I'm going." After ten years of marriage, that's all he said.

I coached the school soccer team as an assistant, and that week at practice, I shared my pain with the coach, who was also our pastor. He'd been incredibly supportive of both Nolan and me during our counseling sessions. So, I wasn't surprised when he texted to check on me two days after Nolan left.

What surprised me that evening was where the text conversation went next. He caught me completely off guard when he told me he had feelings for me. I knew I shouldn't listen. But he told me everything I wanted to hear during those dark and vulnerable days of my marriage. At the time, I didn't consider the fact that he knew exactly what to say. With raw honesty, I had poured myself out during our counseling sessions. When he said that "I was a 'desirous' woman" and that "every man in the church struggles toward me," I couldn't believe what I was hearing. Unfortunately, those words filled a void I felt with my husband, and I let them.

It would never be me. I would never allow something like this to occur. That was my vow to myself. In high school and college, if you had suggested I could ever stray so far from my faith that I would put myself in this situation, I would have laughed. I knew right from wrong. I had learned self-control. I had done all the "right things" to avoid such circumstances. Then, the unexpected moment came, and that's exactly what happened.

I had plans, things I wanted to do for the Kingdom of God. So, when my marriage started to fall apart, and I found myself with feelings for someone other than my husband, I read scripture and prayed daily. I truly wanted a stronger relationship with God, yet I knew I was starting to struggle within myself.

Maybe you've been there too. You've felt the attraction and thought about giving in. Perhaps you've stepped over the line and feel like you have no way back.

You might be on the other side of my story, wondering why I would share it publicly. But honestly, I have to share. I write because no one in the church (or outside of it, frankly) talks about this subject, at least not in a healthy way. We condemn it and judge it, but we never openly discuss how to avoid it or talk about the path to healing once it occurs.

This topic needs to be brought into the light, not as something acceptable and justifiable, but to reveal the truth about how it happens. Anytime we bring sin from darkness into the light, it loses some power. Secrecy gives sin room to spread. I believe this to be a strong reason why infidelity remains such a prominent issue in society. That's why James told his readers to "confess your sins to one another."[1]

My first word of advice to anyone in this situation, even if the infidelity is still only in your mind, is to tell someone you trust. If you find yourself having frequent thoughts about another person, it's time to talk through the reasons why. By bringing it into the light early, you might be able to avoid much of the pain I endured.

Throughout the book, I'll refer to scripture verses and tell you about how my faith helped me survive. I'm still amazed at the beautiful way Christ restored me after I began to understand God wanted better for me. That being said, I'm aware infidelity causes just as much damage to families who don't share my beliefs. If you're in that group, I feel honored that you've chosen to listen to my story—the story of the other woman from a Christian perspective. Regardless of how you feel about faith, I want this book to help you understand the view of the other woman. Hopefully, my journey can inspire someone to choose a better path, whether or not we share the same faith.

That's why I tell my story. I want to help someone else avoid the pain I felt and inflicted on others. I also want to bring hope to those still carrying their shame. No matter what you've done or how unredeemable you believe you are, you can turn things around. And for those who want to explore the faith that got me

---

[1]   James 5:16

through this experience, I want to remind you: Christ will never abandon you. Like the father of the Prodigal Son, He's waiting. I pray my story helps you see that.

PART I

HURT

IT COULD NEVER HAPPEN TO ME

I remember the day I asked Jesus to be my Savior. I was four years old in the back seat of my parents' Chevy Citation. We were on the way home from buying a scooter for my birthday. From that moment on, I planned to live for Jesus.

I went to a Christian school, and by the time I hit my teens, I prayed I could be an example to other kids my age. But that's about the time the atmosphere at the church started to shift. After returning from camp, someone started a rumor that I had snuck out of the cabin with a couple of other girls to meet up with boys—which I did not do—and the pastor fed it. It didn't take long for me to realize I'd been labeled. Other parents had been instructed to keep their sons away from me. I was completely innocent, totally devastated, and experienced my first faith crisis. As a young teenage girl, I didn't understand how this could happen with someone I trusted so much.

Dad and Mom helped start that congregation; they weren't going to change churches. But when I got my driver's license, they gave me permission to switch churches. The church that sponsored my school restored my faith in the church. They helped me grow so much in my last few years of high school. There, several mentors encouraged me, and one very special high school teacher inspired me to go to a Bible College in Wisconsin, where I met Maggie.

Maggie and I quickly became friends and teammates. I would be in awe as she shared her plans to go to the jungles of Africa to live for God and share the gospel. The two of us had made strong commitments to Christ. I thought nothing could shake my faith, but that's because other than those rumors, nothing had ever happened to make me second-guess it.

My friend was only a few months from graduating when a car accident took her life. I wrestled with her death for several years following. Why would God allow something like that to happen to someone who loved Him so much and planned to be a missionary in a developing country? It was terribly difficult, but it forced me to land on what I believed and why.

Set Realistic Expectations

I was still reeling from my friend's death when I met Nolan the following October. Our blind date started with an unusual gift. Because he didn't know me or what kind of flowers I might like, he brought a glass pumpkin with a goldfish swimming in it. I loved the uniqueness.

Things moved quickly after that. In November, instead of going home to Virginia for Thanksgiving, I went to Michigan to meet Nolan's family.

We married a little over a year after our engagement, and from the beginning, things were a bit rocky. About a year into our marriage, I remember driving to a hotel after an intense argument. Nolan had just revealed that the reason he married me was "only because it was what everyone expected us to do next." I sat in the car and prayed, "God, if this is what our relationship is going to be, please don't bring children into this."

Looking back, I can see our problems started while we were still in college. I anticipated him changing, growing, and maturing. It really wasn't fair. Even though I still see the potential within him to become everything he was created to be, it's not reasonable to expect someone to change for you. Perhaps that's my first piece of relationship advice. I don't claim to be an expert, but experience tells me if you can't appreciate someone exactly the way they are, marriage might not be the best route.

Nolan and I worked hard to keep our marriage together. Even after he found out about my affair, we tried counseling through a different church. At that point, though, I believe we both knew how things would end. A few months later, he served me with divorce papers.

The Innocent Stage

I don't think anyone chooses an affair because it's "fun." At least no one I've talked to. Like a person who turns to drugs or alcohol during difficult times, I was looking for a way to alleviate the pain.

For nine years, Nolan and I rode turbulent waves. We'd have seasons that went smoothly. My confidence in our relationship would grow. Then something would happen, and he would break my trust—hidden pornography, smelling like alcohol during a time in our lives when we did not drink, or the lack of spiritual leadership. I had shielded so many from the truth regarding the struggles in our marriage. But after almost a decade, I realized I was the only one in the marriage actually trying to change or fix anything. It was exhausting, and I felt like a failure.

The trip he took that was the final straw wasn't abnormal. It was nothing new for Nolan to call me on the drive from work and tell me he was coming home just long enough to pack a suitcase, and then he'd be gone for whatever timeline his employer deemed necessary. It had been a strain on our relationship ever since the kids were born.

For two years before Nolan left on that trip, I believed the pastor was trying to help me grow and work through my marriage problems. He had become a wonderful friend to both Nolan and me. I hadn't thought anything about it when he asked me to be the assistant coach for the school soccer team. He knew I played in college and would enjoy building relationships with the players.

Playing the flute, heading up the nursery, teaching, singing, and serving in the church helped keep me busy and distracted me from the discontent I felt about my marriage.

Pastor Jim Edwards had counseled Nolan and me several times. We answered the hard questions, and he gave us Biblical advice. However, the cycle of our marriage continued. I truly admired Jim's leadership skills. This was the thing I felt was missing most in my husband. I could see his potential to lead, but he just didn't step up.

Every morning before the kids got up, I took time to pray and read scripture, and I asked God to keep my thoughts pure and make my desires only for Nolan. I was still building my relationship with Christ and wanted to continue growing. Only God could see the struggles in my heart and mind, though. I didn't share these struggles with anyone but Nolan. I believed I was addressing my discontentment in the most appropriate way I knew.

I'm a pretty upfront person—sometimes too upfront. I told him I needed him to be the leader of our family and deepen his relationship with Christ. I even told him I saw those qualities in Jim. But he didn't suggest we change churches, and he didn't change. Looking back, it feels like he wasn't taking the steps to protect our marriage and our family, even after I had been honest about my struggles.

Having appropriate boundaries with someone of the opposite sex is always wise. Yet, at the same time, the friendship between Jim and me grew. He listened, and we talked about everything—soccer, church stuff, kids—but never anything inappropriate. This growing friendship is something I should never have allowed to happen, but I trusted Jim and never doubted my strength to not go down "that" road.

The Door Opened

As I mentioned, when Nolan left after I begged him to send someone else, I knew everything was over. The pain was horrible, and I became susceptible. I didn't recognize it at the time, but I was vulnerable.

When Jim texted on that Wednesday to check on me and inserted the statement, "You know every man in church struggles toward you," I should have turned off the phone and walked away. Instead, I was drawn in as he started to tell me the things my hurting soul needed to hear. I had naturally grown to depend on and trust this man more than my own husband.

Jim had many strong ties to our family. He had been Nolan's youth pastor, and he officiated at Nolan's sister's wedding. I found out much later that Jim had sent me two emails under a different name, an entire year before we crossed the line. They were very suggestive messages that I deleted immediately. I even mentioned them to Nolan. Jim told me later he used them to gauge whether I was ready to move into a relationship. I never imagined those emails were from anyone but a stranger.

Some might want to defend me by saying he groomed me during counseling or that he was the person in power. But I was an adult with my own freewill. I wrongly saw his advances as the answer to all my marriage problems. The realization that my marriage couldn't be saved let me justify my actions and made it easy to give in to the temptation. And after the first indiscretion, it was as if the enemy put a veil over my face, and the reality of it all did not exist.

Everything with Jim only lasted about a month, but it changed everything.

I know, it sounds crazy. But after I crossed that line, I couldn't see the truth. In my mind, my actions impacted no one but me. No one would ever know. My lies, even though they were to myself, isolated me, and I became completely oblivious to the reality surrounding me.

Nolan's leaving, followed by my indiscretion, opened the door to an insane inner battle. In the months that followed, I lost an incredible amount of weight because of the stress of all the lies and secrets. The circumstances had totally overtaken me. I had never been deceitful before. Lying was completely against everything I believed. And now someone I respected was encouraging me and telling me which excuses and untruths to share. I felt relief from the pressure of my failed marriage and complete disgust with myself at the same time.

But it doesn't matter how many lies we tell ourselves, the truth always comes out—always. Your life will follow the choices you make, and sooner or later, everyone around you will know what truly happened in your life as they have in mine.

The Veil

I wish I could say I was seduced or blame someone else for everything that happened, but at the end of the day, I understand that I made a choice that redirected the entire trajectory of the lives of my husband, my children, and myself.

After Nolan found out, things just got worse between us. I considered myself damaged goods, and he became very domineering. This pushed me away even more.

Six months after Jim and I ended things, Nolan filed for divorce. I was so relieved. After what I'd done, I couldn't bring myself to file even though I knew our marriage was over.

At the same time, I was afraid for the future. If not for my children, I may have allowed depression, fear of the future, and anxiety to overtake me. But I pushed forward for their sake.

I had been a stay-at-home mom since my oldest was born, but divorce meant I had to go back to work. I found a part-time job in a financial practice that allowed me to be available for my very young children. I was determined to figure it out. Returning to Virginia to be near family wasn't an option. Nolan was a good dad, and I never doubted his commitment to spending equal time with our children. Our kids needed him as much as they needed me.

I know that in some circumstances, it's better for children to be with one parent. We should never put our children in danger. However, if your children are blessed to have two loving parents, I pray you'll never use them as leverage. It saddens me when I see a parent put their own wants ahead of their children, especially when it means keeping them away from a great dad or mom.

Nolan and I feel very strongly that having both parents equally present in our children's lives is best for them. So, though I had no family close by for support, I decided to survive in Michigan, even if it meant starting from the ground up. And that's exactly what I did by God's grace.

Divorce didn't alleviate the weight of shame and guilt, and Jim didn't make it easy. He contacted me the day after Nolan filed to ask if I would be willing to pursue a relationship since he was getting divorced as well, and I fell into the pit again. He assured me his divorce was coming soon. For three months, the lie of "we're both getting divorced" reinforced my veil.

That's something everyone on both sides of every kind of sin needs to understand. The veil that the enemy puts in front of your eyes when you cross the line is impenetrable. On the other side of the sin, I can see how foolish my actions were, but in the middle of it, I was blind. I believed a man with good leadership skills would be better for my children and me. The happiness I felt in the fleeting moments when I was with Jim convinced me I could create a happier life for myself and the kids with him. The veil provides justification for everything and lets you trust the lies, even when the impact is crushing you and your life is imploding.

With the veil on, it was easy for Jim to lull me into believing we would be together forever. Like a fool, I trusted him once again. However, less than a week after he told me he wanted to call my mom to begin to build a bridge of healing, he told me he was reconciling with his wife.

I've talked to people who have struggled with other unthinkable sins, even crimes, and walked through to the other side. Each one talks about this veil, an inability to see the truth of how their actions will affect their loved ones. If you're considering crossing the line in any area of your life, I want you to be aware of it. After you step one foot into his territory, Satan will put his blinders on you. You will not be able to see the truth, regardless of how strong you think you are and how obvious it seems to those on the outside.

The Problem with Power

The emotional destruction of my indiscretion was heavier than I ever imagined. I continued to drop into those deep, dark emotional valleys, and they affected every part of my life—emotionally, spiritually, and physically. It was easy for the church to believe Jim when he threw me under the bus. No one wanted to think the pastor would lead another person into sin.

Unfortunately, it's not uncommon for pastors to give in to this kind of temptation. And when they do, because of their position and the trust the congregation puts in them, the person in the pew can fall into the trap I succumbed to as well. Jim's position gave me the inner permission to walk through that door. (A quick web search reveals dozens of church-related scandals, and many more get swept under the rug because the church doesn't want anyone to see its faults.)

Sadly, hiding it just makes it worse. It feeds the pastors who thrive on power. They feel untouchable.

It's not a new problem. Throughout history, kings and priests have used their positions to manipulate and satisfy their selfish desires. Not even the Bible is immune to scandals. I wonder if that was King David's problem.

David loved God. A man of faith from humble beginnings, he began as a lowly shepherd but quickly accomplished feats no one would have imagined. He led armies, developed an impressive reputation, and built a special force of over thirty mighty men, including Uriah, the husband of Bathsheba, and Eliam, her father, who became his closest friends.

In 2 Samuel 11, we read about the day David decided he was so powerful that he no longer felt he had to lead his troops into battle. The extra time, combined with the lack of accountability, created a predictable outcome. King David used his authority to coerce Uriah's wife to sleep with him. He went on to abuse his power and wrong two of his closest friends by making arrangements for Uriah to be killed so he could take Bathsheba as his wife. This type of betrayal, though ancient, is very similar to my situation with Jim and many other stories one hears about infidelity.

Sadly, I'm sure many people blamed Bathsheba. She was right there on the roof bathing, and because King David was the beloved warrior who had set Israel free from the Canaanites, Amorites, and Philistines, no one wanted to point a finger at him. In fact, the people revered David so highly that when Chronicles was written nine hundred years later, they left out his indiscretion.

I can't begin to describe the feelings of betrayal Jim left me with. As everything with him came into the open, he made me feel more and more like he got what he wanted and threw me away.

He resigned before the truth came out, telling me it was to shield the church and protect his family. Later, he told his wife and many others that I had a crush on him and had initiated the relationship. When people from the church saw me, they walked in the other direction as if I had a horribly contagious disease. A few of the church leaders told me they couldn't be my friends because I was living in sin.

Though I convinced myself I wasn't hurting anyone but myself, my choices affected so many people I loved. I had hurt and disappointed my parents, my children, my church family, and everyone I knew. The personal and spiritual imbalance followed me for years.

More than 500 miles from family, I felt so alone. In the beginning, secrecy isolated me. I avoided my friends so I wouldn't have to lie to them again. After everything came out about Jim and me, I lost nearly every friend I had made in Michigan. Some who avoided me during those dark days still don't speak to me today.

Regardless of the issues in your marriage, how unhappy you are, or even if your spouse isn't willing to work to resolve the problems, an affair will only make it worse. It's not even a bandage. It's just a hidden addition to the chaos.

02

HOW COULD IT HAPPEN AGAIN?

After saying all that, you might think I learned my lesson after everything came crashing down, but I carried a great deal of pain following the divorce and Jim abandoning me twice. Though I should have turned toward the Great Healer, I chose another path. Jesus would have been happy to walk with me through the hurt, but I wasn't looking to the One who can heal the past as well as the present. Instead, I questioned whether He was even real at all.

The weight I carried seemed to increase. Between the deep emotional valleys and knowing I had hurt and disappointed everyone I knew, I wanted to reject God. Was He really even there? Despite my doubts, my Savior never stopped working in my heart.

After Nolan filed for divorce, I found a job in a local financial office. My new boss, Mark, was kind. Even after he knew my story, he didn't judge or shun me. When Jim would show up at work trying to continue our relationship, Mark didn't blame me.

The new job helped with the pain. Mark became a good friend. We talked about everything; it felt so natural. I told him about my life problems, including the horrible dates I tried to go on, and he made me feel like I had value through my divorce and beyond.

From May through August, while my divorce was being finalized, I worked part-time in Mark's practice. With Nolan and Jim out of my life, I could finally start to pick up the pieces. But then another shoe dropped.

In January, Mark came to my desk and told me he needed to cut my hours. He was "restructuring," which basically meant he couldn't afford to pay me, cutting my already small income even further. I picked up other jobs to make ends meet—substitute teaching, driving the bus, and working the front desk at a local gym. I did whatever I could to provide and stay close to my children.

However, I also believed in Mark's business. I appreciated his vision for the future of his practice. So, for two years, after I worked all day and the kids went to bed, I put in a few hours to help him get back to the place where he could pay me again.

As Mark started to share his own heartaches and struggles, our friendship grew. We told each other our deepest secrets. I learned that part of his money struggles stemmed from his wife not wanting to rein in her spending during his transition. Mark has his own story about the struggles of his marriage, and he shared many details with me. However, it wasn't until later that he told me he had chosen infidelity to escape his pain for years.

Our paths crossed in more places than work. He led scouts, and both of us had children in the troop. I loved that he was so involved in his children's lives. I don't think I've ever met a father so focused on helping his children become leaders. He wrote affirmations in the kids' bathroom and encouraged them every chance he got. He disciplined them, not in a military authoritarian way, but in a Biblical, loving way. I loved the fact that his kids meant so much to him. They were the primary reason he tried to work it out with his ex-wife for so long.

I still remember the day he suggested we go to Applebee's for lunch. Our pasts made it easy for us to move from two people encouraging each other through a difficult marriage and divorce to becoming the secretary who slept with the boss.

The Lies We Tell Ourselves

I knew from the start that Mark never planned to leave his wife. Still, I let myself believe the most popular lies of infidelity: no one will ever find out, we deserve to be happy, we're not hurting anyone, we can trust each other, it's just between us.

For four and a half years, I clung to the time we had together. I loved him. I loved how he listened to me and how he supported his children. I loved supporting and encouraging him. I loved the way he treated me and made me feel like I had worth. That part of my psyche had been so greatly damaged in my previous relationships. Mark became my best friend.

We told ourselves we were simply being there for one another and to give each other some enjoyment in the middle of so much hurt and pain. Still, I was the other woman with no hope of ever having a God-honoring relationship.

It didn't help that Mark was the only person in my life who encouraged me to move forward and better myself. I know this may sound like an oxymoron, but it is the truth. He helped me get my securities licenses so I could earn commissions and quit my other jobs. Plus, he pushed me to get beyond my past. "You are not going to improve yourself and do all you're capable of doing until you stop being Jim's victim." The strong leadership I had looked for in Nolan and Jim, I found in Mark.

I didn't have that kind of encouragement to become a leader growing up. I love my dad, but he ran a dictatorship of sorts, so Mark's encouragement was exactly what my brokenness needed.

On the other side, Mark told me he'd never been his true self in front of anyone before. He'd never felt like he could talk about the hard things until he met me. He had never felt safe enough to share his secrets with anyone until then. He and his (now) ex-wife had polar-opposite opinions on some volatile political issues, but he didn't learn about them until after they married because he wouldn't engage in tough conversations.

I can't count how many times Mark and I talked about stepping away from the physical part of our relationship. He knew he needed to figure himself out and be better for his kids. And I encouraged the break every time he mentioned it. Many times, we actually succeeded in putting a hold on our relationship outside the office. I wanted the best for him; he wanted to be a better man, but we couldn't seem to resist the bond we had.

Every time we were apart, it was a living hell. I knew the truth behind his wife's social media posts and the "show" of their perfect family and herself when we were at the same events. She behaved differently behind closed doors. Like when I was struggling with Jim, I started to have physical reactions to the "nightmare." Feeling like I needed to throw up, I would go to the bathroom and just sit and cry.

During the entire four years, I lived in fear. I asked Mark often, "What if your wife finds out? I'll be left with nothing, Mark."

He assured me everything would be just fine. Mr. Positivity couldn't figure out why I worried so much about it. But Jim had abandoned me, the church turned their backs on me, and Nolan had left. I'd had no one after that whole experience. The fact that he battled between his feelings for me and his loyalty to his family left me confused and afraid. I didn't know how to deal with it. The back-and-forth took a toll.

I don't think anyone realizes the full impact of infidelity. Until I crossed the line, I believed an affair was just something someone engaged in. By the time I understood the mental, emotional, and physical ramifications, the veil kept me from recognizing the truth. I shrank to nothing. My short frame was just skin and bones. But I also shrank in every other aspect of my life. I was not the person I wanted to be, but I couldn't see a way out.

03

CHOOSE YOUR HARD

Anytime we experience pain, we seek a solution. Broken bones take us to orthopedic doctors, toothaches force us to call the dentist, and headaches send us to the medicine cabinet. We face emotional pain the same way. We just want relief from the hurt. Sadly, instead of healthy remedies, most try to bandage their emotional pain with things that look like homemade splints, pulling teeth with pliers, and curing headaches with ice packs.

When life becomes difficult, some resort to working too many hours or finding excuses to stay away from home. Others work out more than usual, turn to alcohol or drugs, overspend for retail therapy, or focus on their children instead of their marriage, and a third group falls into the trap of infidelity. While none of these forms of self-medication can be called healthy, all can become addictions and cause tremendous damage.

Choose Your Hard

Mark and I both knew what we should do, but the veil blinded us. It's hard to explain the view from inside the "other woman" relationship. I'd been raised on the truth, but the pain of my marriage, my first affair, and then the consequences, sent me looking for ways to self-medicate. Worse still, using an adulterous relationship to self-medicate created a virtual reality as believable as the scenes in a VR headset. Unfaithfulness deceives everyone, not just the family and friends we're trying to hide from.

Yes, marriage can be hard. In addition to unrealistic expectations, sometimes the façade your spouse wore while you dated comes off after you say I do, and the change becomes unbearable. Some people—both women and men—find themselves in physically or emotionally abusive relationships. And sometimes things just don't work out as expected, or two people simply grow in different directions.

Whatever the reason, most people do everything they can to avoid divorce. No one wants to tell their family and friends their marriage is struggling. Sharing the fact you're in an abusive relationship—especially for a man—can seem impossible. Facing death seems easier than filing for divorce, especially for those who've gone to counseling and done everything possible to save their marriage.

We Always Have a Choice

Some people like to use the excuse, "I didn't have a choice." But if we're honest with ourselves, we always have a choice.

Every arena in life offers difficult options. Will I eat well, go to the gym, work out, and have sore muscles, or will I let myself go until I can't get off the couch? Will I cook something at home and save money, or will I eat out four times this week and skip my cell phone bill? Will I read a book to better myself, or will I play games on my phone and scroll to pass the time?

Our marriages aren't exempt from the hard choices life presents every day. The key is choosing your hard. Admitting failure and defeat in a marriage is hard, but turning to alcohol and drugs is harder. Walking away from abuse is hard, but living with fear and intimidation is harder. Doing the work of reconciling with your spouse is hard, but living with the regret of not even trying is harder. Divorce is hard, but I can tell you from experience, the fallout from being the other woman is harder.

Many couples struggle because discussing problems with their spouses is hard. Like most of humanity, they avoid talking about some subjects. However, choosing to face the hard parts of those discussions often helps stop the truly difficult. If those "it can't happen to me" situations become a reality in your life, you're ready to face and address them in a healthy way because you chose to discuss them before the temptation.

You might feel, like I did, that no one will understand the emotional and physical hell you're going through. It will feel hard bringing up those topics, but I'm living proof that there are many others who are walking through the difficulties of marriage and infidelity. While no one knows exactly how you feel, more people than you might imagine would be honored if you shared your story and allowed them to walk with you through your healing.

It Can Happen to Anyone

Long before it happens, we all need to acknowledge that we are susceptible to every temptation. Then, we have to decide which hard we will choose and embrace it. This means we strictly refuse to even entertain choices that would tear our families apart, like that of infidelity. Not setting that boundary leaves the choice to chance, and when chance has its way, it chooses what is easiest in the moment. Giving in to temptation with Jim seemed easy in the moment. I had all kinds of reasons to justify my behavior in my head. And after the guilt of the first indiscretion took hold, shame and lies told me I couldn't walk it back.

Had I turned to Jesus during those days, I am confident He would have given me the strength to make my mark in the sand. The Bible promises that God will never let us be tempted beyond what we can withstand. When we are tempted, Christ will provide a way out so that we can overcome it.[2] Many people think the Bible is full of rules, but when you really examine the things Jesus emphasized, including the serious nature of divorce and marital faithfulness, you begin to realize God put the rules in place for our protection.

Jesus wants to help us when life gets hard, but we have to choose His hard—keeping your life in line with scripture even when it's uncomfortable. If we're honest, we can see the value of Christ's hard work in our relationship with our children. We establish rules to protect them from making mistakes or hurting themselves. God does the same for us. Following Biblical instruction is as difficult for us as it is for our kids to follow our rules when they're with friends who want to lead them astray. But the Biblical instruction is every bit as protective.

Living with the Hard You Choose

As you consider your choices, it's important to remember that you will continue to deal with your past choices for years after you make them. Mark and I married two years after he filed for divorce. Still, we deal with the fallout from our affair years later. We continue our healing journey daily.

You need to understand that the people who were hurt because of the hard choices you made sometimes will make choices that hurt you. Your children may act out or struggle to

---

[2]   2 Corinthians 10:13

move past seeing you fall. Friends say things they regret, parents aren't always welcoming, and the community feels awkward.

Most times, they won't intentionally mean to cause you grief. However, just like your choices in dealing with pain affect many, as they process their pain, their choices will ripple over to you.

I felt like Nolan left me and our marriage when he chose to go out of town for work that day. I gave up everything, including my reputation for Jim, and he had walked out, leaving me feeling like collateral damage. After years of trying, I ended up with a huge fear of abandonment. One day, as we were walking and having an intense conversation, I shared that fear with Mark.

"I know I'm going to end up alone again. I'm always the one who ends up alone."

"I'm not Jim," Mark said. When Mark shared these words, I felt my heart and body exhale with relief. I knew then, for the first time, that he and I would be okay even though the way forward was still unknown.

Until we took that walk, I had always kept plan B in my back pocket. I needed a backup strategy. Abandonment issues became part of the "hard" of my choices. They were what I was used to.

Choosing an affair to ease your pain also means your mind is forever changed. Your choice will imprint images and mold memories in your brain —things you can never completely erase. You'll find you have mental battles you didn't experience before you crossed the line. Those battles of the mind are worthy battles. We don't want to fall into that temptation again. That's why we need Christ to lean on as we put our worst hard choices behind us and move forward in faith and forgiveness. If we try to fight them on our own, we will fail.

Exodus 14:14 tells us, "The Lord will fight for you; you need only to be still." If we want to choose the hard that's best for us, the one that will leave us with peace, we need to give the battles of our mind to Christ every single day.

PART II

HOPE

04

DARKNESS TO LIGHT

Mark and I were sitting in my living room, having the hardest conversation in our relationship, when we heard the knock. I peeked out the window. "It's her," I told Mark.

Because we worked so closely together, it wasn't uncommon for Mark to stop by my house on behalf of the business. I'm sure his wife had seen his truck in my driveway before. But this was the first time in four and a half years she thought there might be something between us and had driven by to see if his truck was there.

Mark had recently filed for divorce. The situation at home had reached the point where he believed leaving would be healthier for his children. His decision to leave had allowed us to start planning for a future together. We told ourselves things would be better soon, and everything "wrong" in our relationship could be made right. I finally felt like I could trust again.

But the conversation we were having before that knock revived those guardrails. "I have to try one more time, Laura." I didn't understand. His then-wife's behavior was self-absorbed. She belittled him, didn't let him lead their home, and screamed to get her way, yet he felt like he should try. I trusted him. I'd seen a light in the future we both committed to for ourselves and our children.

Still, I knew the risk existed. I couldn't ignore the fact that we had put ourselves in a position that was not honoring God. After all, though we were making future plans and pursuing a committed relationship, Mark still wasn't "mine."

"Without you in the picture, Laura," Mark finished.

I couldn't breathe. On the outside, I looked strong, but my entire body felt numb. Words can't fully express my pain, but I knew deep in my soul Mark had to work this out for himself. My whole world was falling apart around me as he started talking about how we could move forward separately.

Despite the gut-wrenching feeling, I chose to support him again. "I'll honor your decision."

That's where we were when her knock interrupted.

Mark greeted her at the door, and I walked to the back room so he could talk freely with her.

After a few minutes, Mark called for me. I came out to find them both standing in my living room. *What was she doing in my home? Why did he bring her into my house?* From anger to pain, betrayal, and fear to guilt, my emotions were reeling.

Cheeks still wet from crying, I faced her.

"What are you crying for?" she asked.

"Because I'm trying to do the right thing now."

The most awful moments of my life passed as she listed my flaws, including that I had ruined my marriage. She only knew what most of the community knew: my first marriage ended as a result of an affair, but that's all she needed to know to accuse me. "Stop ruining everyone else's marriages," she yelled.

I was surprised by how calm I stayed after her barrage of berating. "I can't control your perception of what happened in my marriage," I told her. God obviously helped me during those few moments. I knew she deserved to be upset.

I stood there awkwardly as she and Mark had a brief conversation about everything he "needed to take care of" since she had convinced him they should try to make it work after she received the divorce papers. When they finished, he gathered his things and walked out in front of her with his head hanging low.

No goodbye, no closure. He didn't even look my way as he walked out of my life without a word.

The Darkness Closed In

The year prior to his wife coming to my home that day had been a roller coaster. Mark had been facing this inner battle for many years.

It started in November. He had decided to move toward divorce after an evening of listening to his wife scream at the kids once again. He realized that at least that way, his kids would have a peaceful place to go half the time. As family discovered the details of the situation, they backed him as well. Just as he was about to start the process, everything got confusing.

At first, he wanted to wait until after the holidays. Then, his father-in-law ended up in hospice and passed away in early February. In May, they finally had the memorial service. And then just when I thought Mark and I might finally be able to move forward, she convinced him to go to counseling. That's where he shared his desire for divorce because he felt more comfortable bringing it up with a third-party present, since her reactions were unpredictable.

Throughout the time they were seeing a counselor, Mark and I were secretly making plans for our future.

In July, I saw a light at the end of the tunnel when he filed for divorce and told his children. But when you're walking in the kind of darkness I was living in, most signs of light are just reflections of the truth.

One weekend, a few weeks later, something changed. Mark stopped communicating. This was extremely unusual. He was working up the courage to tell me he was going to try to reconcile with his wife.

Again

Losing Mark started a massive downhill slide. Learning to trust him had taken time. Now he was walking out on me, too. I didn't know how to move on. His wife didn't want me working for him for obvious reasons, so I lost my job. After working so hard during the transition and spending so much time getting my insurance and securities licenses, I had to quickly figure out a way to care for my children while I walked through my worst nightmare. I felt like I was experiencing Mark's death.

The darkness only grew thicker when I learned Mark and his wife were planning to purchase the very house he and I had talked about buying together.

Looking for the Light

Everyone says hindsight is 20/20, and when you get to the other side of something like my story, you know it's true. Now, I understand that I created my own darkness during those years. Blind to truth, I couldn't see that placing blame and justifying my actions made everything worse. I questioned God. Why would He allow all this chaos to happen in my life? Was He there? Did God even care about me anymore?

As a girl who grew up going to church every Sunday without fail, I had a strong grasp of scripture. I had been a champion during Bible challenges in my youth. But as I walked through this season, I struggled, questioning and doubting everything I'd learned. Is God really who He says He is?

The questions and the doubts came because I kept hiding everything. I thought if I kept the truth in the shadows, no one would be hurt. And that was the biggest lie.

As long as you keep the lies in the dark, you become completely blind to the truth. Even when someone speaks it directly to you, you can't hear it. Once you cross the line, it's as if you step into a tunnel or a dark cave, and staying there means you see only what you want to see. And it's not just infidelity. With every kind of self-medication, there's a whole world around you—a world full of truth—but all you can see is what's in your VR goggles.

Those who enter into a relationship of infidelity become fully committed to it, even if they aren't exclusively committed to it. They embrace it as normal and don't even realize they're walking in the darkness.

The worst part of deep darkness, whether it's physical or spiritual, is the amount of pain you feel when someone turns on the light. When an affair comes into the light, it humbles a person in a way no one wants to be humbled. And if it doesn't humble you, you need professional help because being found out was the most humiliating experience of my life.

Mindset Change

By the time Mark's wife showed up that day, I had been listening to lies for so long I couldn't separate them from the truth. That kind of thinking rewires your brain.

Ironically, Mark had recommended a book that helped me see the truth more clearly. *The Morning Miracle* by Hal Elrod introduced me to his S.A.V.E.R.S. method, which made a way for me to turn from my destructive behavior.

Elrod recommends we start our day with Silence, Affirmations, Visualization of our best day, Exercise, Reading, and Scribing (writing in a journal).[1] This book helped me want to be better. We naturally have that inclination, but living in the lies can keep us from moving toward it.

Looking back at the books I read and the work I did to get my licenses, I can see that I was striving to better myself in every area of my life, except the part I kept hiding.

That's the first question we need to ask when we find ourselves living a lifestyle we know isn't good for us: Do I want to be better? Whatever addiction you've chosen to alleviate your pain, the first thing you have to do is decide you want to be better. Be honest with yourself. You have to reframe your thinking so you're willing to put your feet behind your choice to be better.

Some people say things like "life is hard, and then you die" or "I'm allergic to hard work." They might be joking, but when we repeat the lies, we start to believe them.

The Bible says, "Be transformed by the renewing of your mind"[3] and "Set your mind on things above, not earthly things."[4] We all need a mindset shift that allows us to see ourselves as Christ sees us. He sees our heart and our potential.

Everything begins in the mind. Affairs don't begin when someone casually compliments you on how nice you look. Affairs begin because of what you're telling yourself outside the circumstances. That's why transforming your mind and setting boundaries are the most vital parts of avoiding destructive forms of self-medication.

The Bible tells us, "No temptation has overtaken you except what is common to man."[5] Don't make the same mistake I did:

---

3   Romans 12:2
4   Colossians 3:2
5   1 Corinthians 10:13

thinking you are exempt because you go to church or know the Bible. "It can't happen to me" or "I would never ___________" are dangerous mindsets. Only a renewed mind that sets clear guidelines before the temptation arises has a chance to resist. That's why having those difficult discussions before anything happens is vital to your marriage and your life. Let me say that again: *It's vital to your marriage and your life to engage in those difficult conversations long before either person feels any kind of temptation.*

Into the Light

During our time of separation, my pain brought me closer to Christ. I started to see God providing for me.

Before I lost my job, we had started the process of transferring to another agency, where Mark would enter into a succession agreement. Out of work, I had a very honest conversation with the owner to see if he had a position for me. I told him about the affair and where Mark and I were in that moment.

Fortunately, at that time in his long-term plan, he needed me more than he needed Mark. I had the administrative knowledge his team needed. God opened that door so I could provide for my family.

Mark struggled internally during those months. He felt crazy turmoil and tried reaching out to me at times. However, I had seen a sliver of light, and I knew I wanted to move toward it. I prayed, "Lord, you have to fight for me. I don't want to keep doing this."

One of my best friends met with Mark and told him, "Listen, you have to leave her alone. She can't move forward if you keep trying to communicate with her." I am still grateful for that gift from God as he used my friend to protect my heart and mind.

After two months of working on their marriage, Mark realized his wife's "changes" were not completely genuine nor long-term.

With years of hiding and lying behind him, he brought all his feelings into the light with his wife and then flew to Florida to spend time with family so he would have a place to think clearly.

That's where he called me from. Even though he'd made a clean break this time, he wasn't sure I would take him back, and frankly, I was scared to do so.

We talked for hours, and Mark brought more truth into the light. He laid out everything—his other indiscretions and other lies he had been telling even me.

Nothing brings healing better than truth. If you're still hiding in the shadows, I want you to know that as hard as it is to admit you've fallen, it's more difficult to keep it hidden. Your friends and family will sense something is up. They may even stop trusting you without knowing why. The stress of holding on to the secret can be excruciating. Jesus wasn't kidding when He said, "The truth will set you free."[6] And that's exactly what it did for Mark, starting that day.

The divorce took three times longer than a normal Michigan divorce, but the eighteen months gave us time to start healing from the deceit and hiding in the shadows. They say the heat of life's challenges reveals the truth about a person, and everything we endured as we began to walk out of the darkness and into the light definitely unveiled the rough places as well as the beautiful spots in our souls. Mark didn't leave his marriage for me. While too many people use it as an excuse after an affair has occurred, Mark truly did leave for his children and his own well-being.

The freedom to work on our relationship again was a scary step at first, but God revealed His plan for us as well.

---

[6]   John 8:32

Embracing Who You Are in Christ

I've been in that place where I told myself, "I've already cheated. I've already been disloyal, why even try?" I understand how that feels.

However, we have to recognize that choosing that mindset is a decision to stay in the past. The good news is that every decision means there's a second option. In this case, it's the option to be better, to treat yourself with the same respect you want for your children, and accept the fact that Christ loves you. Romans 5:8 tells us, "while we were still sinners, Christ died for us." He doesn't expect us to clean ourselves up before he starts loving us.

The Apostle Paul says it best:

If God is for us, who can be against us?

Who will bring any charge against us? Not God, He is the one who justifies.

Who condemns us? No one. Christ Jesus died for us and more than that, He was raised to life and sits at the right hand of God to intercede for us.[7]

No matter what you've done, where you've come from, God loves you.

If you've fallen into temptation and chosen the darkness, God loves you.

If someone has pulled you into the darkness and convinced you that abuse is love, please know God wants something better for you because He loves you.

If you've been conned, and you didn't know the man or woman you've been dating is married, God loves you.

---

[7]   Romans 8:31-34 Paraphrased

You are loved. Jesus wants to bring you out of the darkness and into His light, but you have to choose to believe and move ahead into something new.

05

GOD SEES YOU

As the other woman, I felt alone. I couldn't tell anyone. All my friends thought I was a model Christian, and the shame overwhelmed me. On top of that, self-medication nearly always means we not only have to live with the consequences of our choices, but we also feel the pain of the choices of those around us.

So many times during those years, I faced loneliness and confusion when Jim and Mark tried to do the right thing. I always felt like I had to be the only Christian who let herself get into such a mess.

Over the years, I've learned that's not true. More people than you might imagine hide their story because of the stigma. One of my friends has lived on both sides of the pain. She's given me permission to share her story.

Caryn's Story

Caryn married young and quickly had two children; the youngest had colic, and she was exhausted from the care he required. Her husband lost his factory job just after the second baby was born and took a job at the local fast-food restaurant. While Caryn cared for the house, a toddler, and a screaming baby, her husband's job situation left him feeling dejected and inadequate.

Working in the fast-food industry means supervising a staff of young people. So when the strain of home, coupled with the flirtatious advances of a seventeen-year-old, confronted Caryn's husband, he made some poor choices.

When he came home late, he often blamed the crying baby. When the phone rang, his job needed him to come in. For months, he lived the lie. Caryn, overwhelmed with her responsibilities, never suspected a thing.

When everything came out, Caryn tried to work through the shock, hurt, disappointment, and betrayal. She was willing to put everything behind them and move forward. But her husband allowed the young girl to use guilt to keep him in her life. Caryn finally felt she could be a better parent without the constant threat of the "other woman" and decided to file for divorce.

Being a single mom was hard; her husband didn't engage with his children, and she had to go back to school to be able to provide for them. But Caryn understood it would be a better hard than the psychological turmoil of wondering whether her husband was being faithful.

Never Drop Your Guard

After seventeen years of being a single mother, Caryn remarried, but found herself in the middle of eight years of abuse and infidelity again. But through it all, she held on to Jesus. She now testifies to the way God walked with her during the three long years it took to finalize that divorce. She says, "I couldn't have remained upright through all the loss and changes without the hand of God guiding and blessing me at every turn. He provided grace, courage, and protection as the enemy shot his fiery arrows trying to destroy my faith."

Caryn also appreciated her co-workers as she walked through her divorce. They supported her even after they heard the lies and obscenities. One male co-worker, who had also been a friend for forty years, showed her extreme kindness. He had been having problems in his marriage, and they related to one another.

She wasn't prepared for the relationship to go further. The co-worker became her boss and started showing even more "support." At first, it was just hugs that lingered, and then it became kisses. Finally, it turned into an affair with the reminder that he controlled her employment.

Despite the threat, Caryn admitted the attention felt great. She needed someone to want her.

At the same time, she was still attending church, pretending no one saw what she was doing behind the scenes. But she knew there was one who saw her—God sees all. She'd become the woman she ridiculed.

She knew she couldn't continue. Even if it cost her the job, she had to end it.

> Caryn told me that being the woman who's been cheated on caused deep-seated wounds and emotional issues of doubt and self-worth. But being a woman who cheated with a married man is agony and creates just as many deep-seated wounds and suffering.
>
> Regardless of her situation, God walked with Caryn. She experienced His forgiveness and realized He is gracious and merciful. Caryn said, "I cannot praise God enough for the forgiveness and blessings He poured over my life, regardless of the mistakes I made in this life."

El Roi: The God Who Sees Me

A woman from the Bible also lived with the consequences of others' choices—choices that put her in the position of the other woman. When I heard her story again recently, I heard a phrase that could have helped me as I walked through those dark years.

The story unfolds in Genesis 16. Unlike me, Hagar had been forced into becoming the other woman. In a time when slavery offered no other choice but death, the young woman became Abraham's concubine. And even though the whole ordeal was Sarah's idea, after Hagar became pregnant, she and Abraham's wife didn't get along so well.

Hagar was running away from mistreatment when an angel found her in the desert and told her, "Go back to your mistress . . . The Lord has heard of your misery."[8] Hagar returned to serve Sarah, and from that day forward, she called God "El Roi," the Hebrew words for the God who sees me.

---

[8]   Genesis 16:9, 11

Nothing about Hagar's situation changed that day. The young maidservant was still carrying her master's child. Perhaps she even loved him. She still had to face Sarah every day, knowing she'd been with the older woman's husband, even if it was with permission.

At the same time, everything changed because she had a new perspective on who she was in God. Sitting in that desert after the angel told her to name her son Ishmael, a name meaning "God hears," Hagar said, "I have now seen the One who sees me."[9]

Hagar felt seen by God. She knew she wasn't alone. If only I had been able to embrace that message—Jesus sees me—when I felt abandoned by Nolan. Maybe I wouldn't have looked for something to dull the pain if I had completely understood how God viewed me when Jim said things that made me feel like I had value.

When You Feel Alone

During Mark's and my affair, I dated other men because I knew what we were doing wasn't right. I kept hoping to find the person I could care about more than Mark—someone who would help deliver me from the affair, someone I could have an appropriate relationship with.

But every time the person on the other side of the table started getting serious, I broke it off. I couldn't handle it. Deep down, even though I knew it was wrong, I cared deeply for Mark, and I did not want to hurt anyone else by leading them on. So, even though I knew Mark had made the choice to stay with his family, I ended every other relationship so I didn't drag someone else into our pain.

---

[9]   Genesis 16:13

I know I've never been the wounded spouse, but during those times, it's as if I got a taste of what it was like to be on the other side of the affair—the person I loved was with someone else. Day after day, the affair created an emotional rollercoaster that was mentally, emotionally, and physically exhausting.

As I've grown in my relationship with Christ, I've wondered what kind of words I have for the person left behind—the spouse or fiancé who has felt the sting of being cheated on. I guess I'd first say that I don't feel like I have the right to speak. You didn't deserve to have our choices cause you such pain.

Second, I would say that I'm incredibly sorry. I hate it that I caused another person to feel that kind of pain, and I always will, no matter what the surrounding circumstances might be. But I'm also aware that as much as "I'm sorry" might be what you deserve to hear, it probably won't bring you much comfort as you pick up the pieces. For that, I believe you need to hear the words the angel spoke to Hagar as well.

I wish I could tell every wounded spouse those words, "God sees you." The Almighty is not done with your life. He can take whatever's happened and bring something good out of it if you allow Him. I truly admire Jim's wife. Though I don't know where she is today, during the days after our affair came into the light, she handled the pain in the most constructive way possible. She clung to God and moved closer to Jesus.

Everyone says, "Remember, just take it one day at a time." I'm here to tell you that most weeks, you need to take it one step at a time, one moment at a time. If you've been hurt by an affair, forward movement is the goal, regardless of how small that movement seems.

God knows you. He wants to paint you your own beautiful picture of how mighty He is. And remembering that He sees you will help keep you moving forward. Even if you're facing the consequences of someone else's poor choices, the best advice I've heard is to leave your past exactly where it belongs, in the past. Move ahead knowing the One who loves you hears you, sees you, and has a perfect and beautiful plan for your life if you allow yourself to receive it.

06

SEEN, HEARD, AND ACKNOWLEDGED

At some point in my messy life, I began to see who I had become without Christ. I realized that although I was always His child, I had been running from Him. It was a slow process, but when the truth became real, it shook me. I had been faithful in church and believed in Jesus for as long as I could remember. Perhaps my greatest gift had become the root of my downfall.

Those of us who walked with Jesus from our youth sometimes don't take Jesus' death on the cross as personally. We know Romans 3:23 says, "All have sinned and fall short of the glory of God." And Isaiah 64:6 tells us, "all our righteous acts are like filthy rags." However, because human standards tell us we're "good people," sometimes we gloss over those verses and forget they apply. That's where I was before my affair; I couldn't clearly see my sins. Even though I knew my life was better with Jesus, I had never come face-to-face with why I needed Him.

Being the other woman reminded me that my actions were leading me toward spiritual death—the Bible says, "for the wages [penalty] of sin is death"—and that Jesus Christ died to give me the gift of eternal life—"but the gift of God is eternal life in

Christ."[10] It humbled me to realize God loved me enough to forgive me even before I recognized his gift. "But God demonstrates his own love for us in this: While we were still sinners, Christ died for us."[11]

Not everyone goes to the extent of having an affair or giving in to their addictions to learn the truth, but every Christian who has found depth in their faith and learned to love without judgment has been hit with the reality of who they are in their sinful nature. Getting there is different for every person, but without that understanding, you can never move into the fullest life possible.

Jesus Meets Us Where We Are

In John 4, we read about Jesus' encounter with "the other woman." Today, the world knows her only as the Woman at the Well, or the Samaritan Woman. Like me, she let shame dictate her movements. Since women in her time had no rights to initiate a divorce, we know she'd already been rejected and abandoned by five men. I can only imagine the lack of self-worth she felt daily. I'm sure that was the catalyst for becoming the other woman for man number six.

Because of that reputation, she came to draw water when the sun was high in the sky, the time of day she could be certain she wouldn't run into anyone. So, she was probably extremely surprised to see Jesus sitting there alone during the hottest part of the day.

I don't think it's a coincidence that the woman found Jesus at the well.[12] He could have easily walked into town with his disci-

---

[10]   Romans 6:23
[11]   Romans 5:8
[12]   John 4:1-22

ples to get out of the sun. Instead, He chose to wait for her there. And He chooses to be where we are as well. Though I looked for other ways to escape my pain for a time, I found my Savior standing there waiting when I decided to turn away from my addiction and look to Him for healing. As a young girl, I learned that Jesus never moves because He is always the same. When we feel far away, it's because we have chosen to walk away and separate ourselves from Him. This means he's waiting for you to turn back to Him.

Many people avoid coming back to Jesus because they don't want to face the condemnation. But this woman's story helps us see that's not how Jesus works.

The first thing the Savior did when He saw the woman was initiate a friendly conversation. "Would you mind giving me a drink?" In an era when Jews didn't speak to Samaritans, men didn't acknowledge women, and no one looked at someone living in adultery, Jesus saw her, spoke to her, and listened to what she had to say. Though she didn't realize it yet, Jesus already knew her living situation. His actions demonstrated that she was forgiven even before she acknowledged her problem.

Jesus gives you and me that same gift; we simply have to accept it. A prayer that asks for forgiveness shows our remorse; however, Christ offers it before we know we need it. Regardless of what your lifestyle looks like right now, you are already forgiven. You simply have to accept the gift.

Be Honest with Yourself

Aside from water, Jesus asked only one thing of the woman. He wanted her to be honest with herself.

As I mentioned, Jesus approached the woman even though he already knew her living situation. But when confronted, she tried to hide her shame. "I have no husband," she answered. While that was the truth, it wasn't enough truth to set her free.

That's one of the first things I had to do to start my healing process. I had to be honest with myself. It's impossible to heal when you're telling yourself a lie. A person with cancer can't make it go away by denying it exists, and the disease of sin won't heal by ignoring it either.

We each create a narrative for our situation, and most of the time, especially when we're involved in some sort of sin, we believe our narrative is the truth. Your brain is easily reprogrammed to believe whatever you keep telling it. But believing the lie doesn't make it true. It might seem to make it easier in the moment, but it will never make it true.

Even though I knew in my heart I was wrong and felt the shame that brings, it wasn't until I rejected the lies in my mind that I could step into healing. Some people have to hit rock bottom to acknowledge that they need truth. Healing can't begin until we choose to embrace honesty and own our part in whatever separates us from God.

My healing has no precise starting line. It transpired over time, one minuscule right decision at a time. For years, I kept choosing the wrong hard because it was easy in the moment. But the saying, "If it seems too good to be true…" applies to life decisions as well as financial ones. Making the first right decision, even though it seemed tremendously hard, made the next one a little easier. And with every good decision, I moved a little closer to God.

Those first decisions that take you towards change are the most important. You can't build on something you don't start.

Those first steps don't mean you'll be able to see the end clearly or that you'll never go backwards. Every day, people walk through crazy stuff. Sometimes, they even recognize it's crazy stuff. Still, they reject the things they know bring peace that passes understanding. The key is to keep moving forward, just do the next right thing, and remember: three steps forward and one step back is still two steps in the right direction. As much as I wanted to reject God and believe He wasn't there, my heart knew differently. And as hard as it was, I kept moving forward. Progress was slow, but every step was progress.

Broken People

It's important to remember that we live and move among broken people. Nolan, Jim, Mark, his ex-wife, me, and now our children—we're all broken. I've learned that all I can do is my best. I'll never do it perfectly, but I want to do my best to give my all and put Christ first in my life and in my relationships. He is the only one who can navigate my brokenness. He's also the only one who can help me see others in light of their brokenness.

Broken people will hurt us. It helps to keep in mind that hurt people hurt people. No one is born with a desire to make others miserable, but after being hurt again and again, some people act in destructive ways.

However, until you recognize your brokenness and own your sin, you won't be able to see that other people are broken too.

After Mark and I took total responsibility for our parts in our divorces and began actively pursuing our relationships with Christ, we were able to see the other players in our chaos in a whole new light. We realized that Jesus created beauty from our ashes, and He wants to do the same in others' lives.

This new view allows us to respond to attacks from others with love rather than retaliation, even when it's tempting to do so. Before we took on this outlook, every hurtful move our former spouses made felt personal. But when we see them through the lens of brokenness, we no longer see monsters; we see pots waiting for Kintsugi. That's the Japanese art of repairing broken pottery with powdered gold or silver mixed with lacquer. The cracks become part of the pot's beauty rather than its worst flaw.

When you have to deal with mean-spirited, self-focused individuals, remember to see them through the eyes of brokenness. They are dealing with their own personal insecurities. Give yourself permission to set up healthy boundaries, then pray for them and let God change you through your relationship with them. We know Mark's ex-wife still hurts, but we pray for her daily and for her to look to Christ for healing as well from all that has happened.

Jesus Knows the Truth, and He Forgives Us Anyway

Think about how the Samaritan woman must have felt when she realized this stranger knew all about her before He said a word. Everyone knows John 3:16 ("For God so loved the world He sent His only Son . . ."), but did you know John 3:17 says, "God did not send His Son into the world to condemn the world, but to save the world through Him?"

Jesus knew everything about the Woman at the Well, and He knows all about you. Still, He does not condemn you when you come to Him for the forgiveness we all desperately need. In fact, he freely offers that forgiveness. But it's a gift you have to accept, unwrap, and appreciate.

The Messiah wanted the woman to understand that her Heavenly Father loved her desperately. He wanted her to find the path to salvation, to freedom. And He wants that for you.

Like the Woman at the Well, I felt the shame that accompanied my choices and the rejection of my community. But Jesus met me where I was and allowed me to see myself through His eyes—broken but loved, a sinner but forgiven, shunned by friends but accepted by my Savior.

One of the greatest mysteries of the gospel, as the apostle Paul called it, is the fact that Jesus offers forgiveness as a gift. Ephesians 2:4-5, 8 says,

> You were dead in your transgressions and sins, in which you used to live … All of us lived among them at one time, gratifying the cravings of our flesh, … deserving of wrath. But because of his great love for us, God, who is rich in mercy, made us alive with Christ even when we were dead in transgressions … For it is by grace you have been saved, through faith—and this is not from yourselves, it is the gift of God—not by works, so that no one can boast.

I don't have to work for His forgiveness or salvation; the Creator of the Universe gives me both because He loved me even while I was in the middle of my mess.

But like all gifts, to receive and enjoy it, we must open it. In the case of God's grace, that means confession and repentance—a churchy word that simply means turning our back on our sin.

1 John 1:9 says, "If we confess our sins, He is faithful and just to forgive us our sins and purify us from all unrighteousness." A simple prayer of confession, owning everything we've done, is all it takes to open the gift.

The mystery culminates in Romans 10:9: "If you declare with your mouth, 'Jesus is Lord,' and believe in your heart that God raised him from the dead, you will be saved."

If you're still living in shame and rejection, I pray you'll turn around, look at Jesus, and call Him Savior. He's just waiting for you to come to Him, accept His forgiveness, and see yourself through His eyes of love.

07

FORGIVEN, REDEEMED, AND RESTORED

When my affairs came into the light, my shame and guilt multiplied. I didn't need the stares and whispers; I was already beating myself up for going against what I knew was right. And those who outwardly judged me made me assume everyone I met was, too.

Still, I didn't have it as bad as the woman in John 8. No one pulled me out of bed in the wee hours of the morning and dragged me in front of a group of pious church leaders who didn't seem to notice their law said the man and woman both were supposed to be punished. Where was he anyway?

On the other hand, I know what it's like to have the man who says he loves you allow you to face the mob alone.

Adultery is frowned on in today's society, but during Jesus' day it was a stonable offense. Imagine being half-dressed, standing before a huge group of religious leaders, along with a man they called Rabbi. I'm certain the woman never looked up. Perhaps silent tears fell as she stood before her accusers. She probably thought her life was over.

For years, I believed I was beyond saving. Although I never gave up on Christ, and deep down I knew He wouldn't give up on me, I still felt judged, condemned, and sentenced.

When You Feel Condemned

If you feel like the woman from John and me, I have good news for you. Jesus came to redeem you. He sees your beauty and your worth. You are invaluable to Him.

The leaders brought the woman to Jesus to force His hand. They knew He was quick to forgive those with a repentant heart, but what would He do when confronted with rules handed down from the Almighty Himself?

As always, Jesus surprised them. Instead of immediately passing sentence, He bent down and started to write in the dust.

Many have speculated what He wrote there. Did He create a list of sins He knew the men had participated in? Was it a list of men the woman had slept with—maybe even the names of a few in the crowd? Or did He begin to write scripture:

"If my people … will humble themselves… I will forgive their sins …"[13]

"With the Lord, there is forgiveness."[14]

"I will forgive the remnant I spare."[15]

"Though your sins are like scarlet, they shall be white as snow."[16]

---

[13] 2 Chronicles 7:14
[14] Psalm 130:4
[15] Jeremiah 50:20
[16] Isaiah 1:18

The men didn't seem to pay much attention to what he was writing; they kept bugging him, "What should we do with this woman? We caught her. We know she's guilty. Come on, Jesus. It's time for her sentence."

Finally, after what must have seemed like an eternity to the woman, Jesus stood and spoke the words we all know so well, "Let any of you who is without sin be the first to throw a stone at her."[17] And he went back to writing.

The oldest man in the crowd dropped his stone first. With her head still bowed in shame, I wonder what the woman thought when she started to hear the slow thump, thump, thump, thump of rocks falling to the ground. Each one must have been a sound of relief.

I wish more people in the church would take Christ's words to heart. He told those men that her sin was no worse than any sin we harbor in our lives, even the sins that many times, others can't see. Maybe if more people exhibited this truth, I wouldn't have felt like all eyes were on me when I walked into worship with my children after my marriage fell apart. My kids needed to be in church.

I understand they were trying to follow the Bible. Most church people follow Matthew 18:17, where it says to treat someone who refuses to repent like a pagan. Sadly, they miss the few verses that come before it, which talk about walking with someone through their sin and winning them over. And in that moment of my life, I needed the body of Christ to embrace 1 Peter 4:8: "Above all, love each other deeply, because love covers a multitude of sins."

With my parents and siblings hundreds of miles away, those people had become my family. Before the affair with Jim, one of the deacon's wives treated me like a daughter, and some of my closest friends' children called me 'aunt'. But in a small town,

---

[17] John 8:7

everyone knows everyone's business, and many times, I felt like the people I once considered brothers and sisters were holding onto the stones, just waiting for an opportunity to throw them. Losing them was devastating.

Ignore the Crowd

It's difficult to ignore the looks and the ghosting, but that's what Jesus invited the woman to do. When the last man had left the circle, Jesus stood, looked her in the eyes, and asked her, "Where are they? Who has condemned you?"

For the first time since she'd been presented to Jesus, she raised her eyes and looked around. "What just happened here?" I'm sure she wondered.

Amazed, she answered, "No one, sir."

And then Jesus spoke the words He often speaks to me, "Then I don't condemn you either. Go, and leave your life of sin."[18]

Before she could say a word, Jesus forgave her. All she had to do was accept His indescribable gift. That acceptance might be the hardest thing we do when we're walking through the chasm of sin. Is that what David calls the Valley of the Shadow of Death—those days we walk outside of Christ's light, so close to total separation from God it feels like dark shadows could easily swallow us?

Jesus invited the woman to forget about what the crowd thought and focus on His perspective. The Pharisees saw a woman living on both sides of infidelity. Jesus saw a child of God in need of forgiveness.

And that's how He sees you and me.

---

[18] John 8:10-11

Maybe if I'd understood this story then, as I do now, I would have accepted God's forgiveness. Instead, I ran from Him because of the things I had done.

Jesus freely offers forgiveness to everyone willing to leave their life of sin and move forward with Him. He's writing things like, "You are loved," "You are forgiven," "You are worthy."

Those people giving you dirty looks—don't worry about them. They will eventually figure out they don't have what it takes—perfection—to be judge and jury. The only opinion that matters is Jesus', and He has declared you not guilty.

Not Simply Forgiven

Forgiveness is a beautiful gift. After we realize how much we truly don't deserve to have Christ die for us, accepting God's forgiveness lifts huge weights. But God said he wanted to go beyond forgiveness. In 1 Peter 5:10, we read, "And the God of all grace, who called you to his eternal glory in Christ, after you have suffered a little while, will himself restore you and make you strong, firm, and steadfast."

God wants to restore you to a full relationship with Him.

Do you remember David, the adulterer, liar, conniver, and murderer? He'd gotten pretty confident when there were no repercussions for his actions. He thought he'd gotten away with it, but as I said, the truth always comes out. Never forget that! It may take years, but it will come out.

Shortly after the baby was born, Nathan, the prophet, visited and called him out. One of David's greatest attributes is his willingness to own his mistakes. The moment he realized God wasn't pleased, David said, "I have sinned against God."

Like all sin, David had to suffer the consequences for his actions; however, Nathan told him, "The Lord has taken away your sin." And after they mourned the loss of their baby, they had a second son, whom they named Solomon. But because God wanted David to know his sin was behind him, God told them to also call this baby Jedidiah, which means loved by the Lord.[19]

God used this son to remind him that His heavenly Father still loved him and wanted to bless him. He restored David to his place as "a man after God's own heart."[20]

Restoration

God wants to give us that same kind of restoration.

Life often becomes heavy. We carry burdens, challenges, family hardships, shame, loneliness, and marital struggles. Everyone carries something, but when you carry it for too long, it becomes difficult and sometimes too much to hold.

For a very long time, shame kept me from sharing my story, but telling it, along with the way God continues to reveal His grace and love, helps me walk in a restored relationship with my heavenly Father.

Perhaps you've felt the weight of shame and guilt as well as the emotional destruction. In my life, it quickly became heavier than I ever imagined.

The weight is even heavier if you're the wife or husband who just learned that their spouse has been involved in an affair. Maybe my story has been painful to listen to. Plus, if the other person was someone you know or looked up to, the disappointment or hurt might be heavier than you can bear.

---

[19]   2 Samuel 12:13-24
[20]   1 Samuel 13:14

Lay Down Your Burden

David betrayed two of his closest friends, the woman at the well faced tremendous rejection, and the woman caught in adultery lived with tremendous shame. Each carried unbearable weight.

What about you? What kind of weight are you carrying today? It's impossible to do anything bad enough to keep you from experiencing true freedom in Jesus Christ.

Romans 8 continues:

Who can separate us from the love of Christ? Shall trouble or hardship or persecution or famine or nakedness or danger or sword? No, in all these things we are more than conquerors through him who loved us. For I am convinced that neither death nor life, neither angels nor demons, neither the present nor the future, nor any powers, neither height nor depth, nor anything else in all creation, will be able to separate us from the love of God that is in Christ Jesus our Lord.

Jesus is standing there ready to forgive your sin, heal the pain, and help you live the life He intended for you. I pray you will release the chains and take a step closer to Jesus today. That's where hope and healing begin.

It reminds me of the Crowder song "Come as You Are," which he sings for the hopeless and those who have strayed.

Come find your mercy, Oh, sinner come kneel
Earth has no sorrow That heaven can't heal

. . .

Oh, wanderer come home; You're not too far
So lay down your hurt, Lay down your heart, Come as you are.

PART III

HEALING

08

FOR THOSE AFFECTED BY THE FALLOUT

Maybe you picked up this book to try to understand why your spouse chose infidelity, or you have a friend who has been hurt by a cheating spouse. Perhaps it was your father or your mother who was the other man or the other woman. If so, thank you so much for reading this far. I pray that what you've read hasn't caused you even more pain.

No matter which side of infidelity you fall on, it changes you. Infidelity disrupts everything. You will have scars. Give yourself permission to acknowledge them. The pain can affect you in ways you are completely blind to until you're on the other side of the grief. Unfaithfulness deceives everyone, and the pain of betrayal heals on a different timetable for every person.

The pain and the scars can eventually become gentle reminders of God's strength in your life and His power to bring you through the hardest moments. When you face other difficult days, weeks, months, or years, they can help you remember that you survived.

We Cause Pain for Our Children

As much as I tried to protect my children from my indiscretions, they were affected. In both affairs, children on all sides were impacted. If you're the child, and you feel like you're caught in the middle, hold on to the fact that, regardless of what's happening, your parents' love for you will never change. I know, better than most, how your parents' decisions can turn your world upside down, and it might take them a while to be themselves again, but they will get there. They're doing their best. The dark days won't last.

I feel grateful that my own children were willing to forgive me. There were so many times as I walked through this valley that my kids were all I had. All but one or two of my friends abandoned me, and even those who stood by me had lives of their own. My kids had to watch me go through so much—I lost my job and my income. I remember sitting on my porch, feeling like I was just existing. My children had to watch it all unfold, even though they had no idea what was going on at the time.

After Nolan filed for divorce, everything was a mess. One day, as I sat in my recliner crying, only my youngest was home. His older siblings were at school. The two-year-old grabbed some tissues and brought them over to "take care of me." Regardless of their age, your children feel your pain and want to show their love.

Another day, during one of the times Mark and I were apart, the kids and I ran into him and his family at a festival. As we walked around the rest of the day, my oldest, who was twelve at the time, but already taller than my small frame, kept his arm around me. He didn't know why, but he sensed I needed him to take care of me in that moment. My children had to endure things they shouldn't have had to go through.

And if you've been involved in unfaithfulness, your children are in the same boat. It's vital to recognize that they see everything, even what we try to hide, and that this affects them and can influence who they become.

A couple of years ago, my daughter, about twelve at the time, told me, "I just want you to know that I think you and Mark argue well." I had no idea she'd heard Mark and me going back and forth about something the night before. She told me she recognized that, although we were upset with each other, we gave each other space to speak and we listened while the other one talked.

I'm very encouraged that she sees the value in sharing feelings and respecting the other person at the same time. I'm also thankful that my kids get to see me happy again, still struggling, but in healthy ways.

We Cause Pain for Our Extended Family

Emotions run high when relationships become complicated, with or without infidelity. It's easy to take sides or find reasons to blame. When I speak to people who feel like they're on the outside looking in on people they love who hurt, I encourage them to pause. There's always more happening than what you see or even what you're told.

I know I let my parents down. They raised me better. But I didn't need their condemnation—I was giving myself enough of that. I needed their presence.

Anger and disappointment are natural responses. However, in the middle of the devastation and uncertainty, your fallen family member needs you to just be there—to listen without sharing an opinion unless they ask for one. Additionally, if your family member's spouse wants to have a conversation with you, especially if he or she is the one who cheated, I recommend approaching it with the attitude that there's always truth in the middle.

You have every right to whatever feelings your child's behavior or the actions of their spouse stir up. However, if you can be a sounding board or a support to lean on, rather than a voice of condemnation and reason, you can be part of the healing process.

We Cause Pain for Our Church Family

It's especially difficult when we find out someone in the church has been caught in an affair, even more so when one of the people is the pastor. For some reason, we view three of the commandments more harshly than the rest. Judging comes second nature to us when we hear the words steal, murder, and adultery.

However, when someone in our church family crosses one of these lines, they need more love than ever before. I beg you, please don't turn and walk away. Instead, listen without judgment. Take time to hear the person's heart. You don't have to condone their behavior; however, it's healthy for us to remember that anyone can fall into sin.

I know I may never comprehend the pain I caused for those within the church family I truly loved so much. Looking back, I can see how devastated they must have been to have two people they trusted betray them so blatantly. My actions were so terribly selfish. Like a drug addict, I only thought about how to numb my pain, and didn't consider how it would affect those around me, including the church. I wish they could understand the horror I felt within knowing I was causing their pain.

I know the congregation was only doing what they thought was best, but when we look at those who've fallen through the eyes of "That could very easily be me," we can carry out James' message: "Remember this: Whoever turns a sinner from the error of their way will save them from death and cover over a multitude of sins."[21]

---

[21]   James 5:20

We Cause Pain for Ourselves

Much of the pain we inflict upon ourselves when we choose to put on the blinders and pretend we're not hurting anyone else comes when we have to face our parents, children, and friends after the truth comes out. Those church friends I lost still don't speak to me. The pain can feel unbearable. But when those we love start to ask questions, we have to choose our hard again.

It can be difficult to face the truth with the people we care about, but it's harder to defend our actions and justify our behavior. You may have stepped across the line because life with your spouse had become unbearable; however, freedom comes when we don't let that become an excuse. Instead, we just own our part.

It's humbling to admit that we should have handled things differently. When everything happened with Jim, I could have easily said, "My marriage had problems," "He groomed me," "He told me what I wanted to hear," "He took advantage." But all that truth didn't negate the bigger truth: I made the decision. I could have said no.

I didn't realize it at the time, but stepping forward in humility and owning my part in the chaos was the first step to freedom. I've seen others walk through similar circumstances who chose to place blame. Some weren't even unfaithful, but they refused to acknowledge the role their behavior might have played in potentially pushing the other person away. In each case, many who refused to humbly own their mistakes are now repeating them, or worse, those who weren't unfaithful before walked into infidelity themselves.

Humility meant I allowed people to ask any question, and that included my children. Obviously, I had to make my answers to my young children age-appropriate; however, I refused to lie to them or sugarcoat the truth I felt I could share. As they've aged and come to understand more grown-up things, there have been points where they've come back with new questions. Each time, I answer as truthfully as possible for their current maturity.

I believe that being honest with your children about your mistakes opens the door for them to come to you with their own screw-ups later in life. Your honesty will inspire them. "If Mom or Dad owned their mistakes, I know they'll love me when I own mine."

The Pain of the Social Problem

I wish infidelity weren't such a huge social problem. So many people have been touched by infidelity, either directly or indirectly. Most people don't want to talk about it, but the secrets leave stains and scars.

Whether you're the spouse who wants to reconcile, the one left after divorce, the family, or even the community disillusioned by someone you respected, I feel horrible that you have to experience the ache of picking up the pieces of life. But I know it's worse when you have to heal in the shadows. That's why I want to help people bring their pain into the light.

Not only does talking about it help the ones impacted by the affair to heal more quickly, but hopefully, those who think they are immune to the addiction of infidelity will also become aware and build hedges of protection around themselves and their families. If you feel like you need to escape your relationship, decide today that you'll remove yourself from the situation before you fall into temptation.

You may end up getting counseling or reconciling, or you may have to walk through the pain of divorce. I assure you, any of those choices will be a much easier "hard" than the hard of becoming "the other person."

THE FUTURE OF THE OTHER WOMAN

My life was rocky to say the least, but my choices didn't make everything better. They caused me to question my faith and wonder where God was. Despite my doubts, it's clear now that God never stopped pursuing me. He cared for my children and me. He met our needs and showed Himself faithful throughout that challenging time. Though I couldn't see it at the time, God proved Deuteronomy 31:6 to be true: "Be strong and courageous. Do not fear or be in dread of them, for it is the Lord your God who goes with you. He will not leave you or forsake you."

Embracing that knowledge will be essential as you move forward in healing.

A Way Forward

The healing process following an affair has many sides. Yes, those impacted need special consideration; however, the people involved, both men and women, require great healing as well. I truly want everyone to understand that. As much pain as those affected by an affair will feel, the participants have endured at least as much.

The pain of conflict and perhaps abuse sends us out looking for a way to self-medicate, and then we deal with the torment of guilt and shame. When the sin comes into the light, an entirely new form of affliction hits, and even if the infidelity started as a result of verbal or physical abuse or we felt abandoned, most of us believe our indiscretion robs us of our right to defend our feelings.

The person involved in an affair loses much more than most people understand. In addition to friends, reputation, and community, they sacrifice dignity, self-confidence, and trust. Even when they have purposefully decided to live a life of integrity moving forward, they are still left to heal on their own; they never feel free to share their story, and most people live in secrecy for the rest of their lives.

Some involved in an affair will have to watch the person they've grown to love return and reconcile with their spouse. They'll have to recognize that, whenever possible, reconciliation is the best thing and move forward with new wounds.

Whether you've been left alone or you're walking forward with the person you were involved with, it's vital that you move into the next phase of your life with Jesus. Perhaps you're thinking, "You don't know what I've done." You're right. I don't. But Jesus does.

One of the small gifts God gave me right after my first affair was the second pastor who counseled Nolan and me before our divorce. After we each shared our stories, the pastor looked Nolan in the eye and said, "What makes you any better than her?" The pastor tried to help Nolan see how easy it would have been for him to fall into the same situation, and that he had self-medicated, too, by running away from the problem.

God knows about every indiscretion, and He loves you anyway. He's already forgiven you. He's waiting for you to accept His offer so He can make you new and whole. 2 Corinthians 5:17 says, "Therefore, if anyone is in Christ, he is a new creation: The old has gone, the new is here!"

Our Savior continues to make us new as we give Him the things in our lives that hold us back and weigh us down—sins no one else may know about but Him. You don't have to know what the next step looks like, but it's important to take the next right step—a step that takes you closer to Jesus.

What Ifs

You might be asking, "What if the other person refuses to see what they're doing is wrong?" It's true, you will encounter some who feel no remorse for their actions. They will never own their part, and the affair will always be someone else's fault. You'll feel like they are anti-God and anti-family. The only thing you can do for this group is pray for them. They need God to speak to their hearts and bring them to repentance. You are never responsible for someone else's response.

Looking back, it's easy to see how things might have turned out differently if any human in our stories had made adjustments. If Nolan had seen himself the way I saw him, we would never have confided in Jim and opened the door to that relationship. On the other hand, if I had put boundaries in place long before anything happened, Nolan and I may still have divorced, but I wouldn't have had to live with the shame of my actions.

If Mark's ex-wife had seen in him the leader and innovative entrepreneur I saw, and refrained from belittling, yelling, and trying to intimidate him, he probably would have stayed with her. He honestly tried several times, but he felt like he could never live up to her expectations, especially financially. Still, if we'd both decided to live in a way that honored God's word, we would have probably still married, but we would have been able to walk with our heads held high.

I only say that to help those who don't want to follow my path. You have options. I can't change my past; I can only learn from it. I want you to understand that you can make choices that will lead to a more peaceful, confident outcome.

I'm Mark's third wife. Yes, we are aware of the statistics surrounding that number, but we also know how far we've both come in Christ. Today, we each focus on our personal relationships with Jesus, and then we work to make Him the center of our marriage and family.

Our healing journey has taken us through a period of reconciliation—not with humans, but with our Creator, whom we let down.

Becoming the other woman was the hardest thing I could have ever chosen for myself. People ask me if I regret my decision. I regret my decision to sin against God, Mark's wife, their family, and myself. While we praise God for bringing us together, we both regret the path we took to get here. We hate the way it happened.

It doesn't matter how bad your marriage feels; an affair will never be the best way out.

Together, Mark and I want to change the world by showing people, even those in the church, that a life of infidelity is not one anyone has to live. Yes, God can create something beautiful from every choice we make. Romans 8:28 shares His promise: "For those who love God, all things work together for good" (ESV). However, just because God can use our sin and turn it into something beautiful doesn't mean we shouldn't avoid causing pain whenever possible.

We know our story would be even more beautiful without those years of walking in the dark. How much better would it be without the scars of those years?

I wish I could help people somehow feel the intensity and trauma of being the other woman for just five seconds. That's all it would take. If you could feel that pain for just a moment, you would avoid it at all costs.

Mark and I tell people, "If you're thinking about having an affair, come talk to us." We want our story to be a warning to protect as many as possible from choosing a similar road. Don't think it can never happen to you, and don't even test the waters because there's no easy way out. Just because God can bring beauty from ashes doesn't mean he wants us to walk through the fire that caused those ashes.

As a teen and a young mother, I never imagined I would walk this path, but through it all, God never changed my desire to love and impact people. My passion is to help others find healing in the midst of whatever hard choices they have made, to ease the pain of those touched by those choices, and bring restoration to families impacted by these skewed decisions.

But even more, I want to bring glory to Jesus Christ. He has changed my life. I continue to fail daily, yet Jesus loves me. I'm still a mess, but my Savior smiles when He sees me. He willingly went to the cross knowing I would take His great gift for granted and walk away for a time. And when I recognized how much I needed to come back to Him, He stood there with arms wide open. And He waits for you in the same way.

Regardless of where you are in your life, whether you've never really been in church before or you have heard about the love of Jesus since birth, I want to remind you He has a place for you. Paul told Timothy, even "if we are faithless, He remains faithful."[22] If you feel unworthy, as if there's no way you can stand before such a loving God, you're in good company. Every single person who has a deep relationship with Jesus has felt the same way at least once. It's that realization that allows us to love Him as we should.

That's the place I had to get to in order to understand His deep love for me. It's that realization that lets me praise Christ for loving me and raising me out of the pit of being the other woman.

---

[22]   2 Timothy 2:13

WHERE DO WE GO FROM HERE?

As you move forward in hope and restoration, I want to remind you of a few tips I've found that help me stay on the right side of the line. This isn't just the line of infidelity. It's any line that takes you off the path of amazing blessing Christ has laid out for you.

1. Have the difficult conversations BEFORE temptations occur.
2. Talk to a trusted friend or counselor (preferably of the same gender). Don't keep the secrets even if they're still only in your mind.
3. Be honest with yourself.
4. Choose your hard, keeping in mind every hard has consequences. Which consequences will negatively impact you and others the least?
5. Constantly renew your mind with scripture, sermons, podcasts, books, and prayer.
6. Don't test the waters.

And if you do test the waters:

7. Remember that you can't control how others react to the truth.
8. Own your part.
9. Accept Christ's forgiveness and remember God loves you even when you aren't walking where you should.
10. Pray for everyone involved.

ENDNOTES

i   Elrod, Hal. *The Miracle Morning (Updated and Expanded Edition): The Not So Obvious Secret Guaranteed to Transform Your Life (Before 8AM)*. Dallas, TX: BenBella Books, 2023.

ACKNOWLEDGMENTS

To my incredibly supportive husband, Mark, who never allowed me to make excuses or quit following my dreams, who pushed me to pursue them from the very beginning of our friendship years ago. You believed in me when no one else did. You lead me towards Jesus daily, and I will always be grateful to Him for the gift of having you in my life. Thank you for looking to Jesus and allowing Him to change you as well. Your love and outlook on life drive me to be better every single day.

To my tenacious and understanding children: You have loved me and been the rocks that held me together on my darkest days. Because of you, I kept moving and pushing myself to show you that survival is possible even when we make wrong decisions and go through difficult times. I wouldn't give up because I had each of you. God has brought us through more than these pages can express, and I pray that you will always look back and remember how He always cared for us. Each of you brings pride, joy, and encouragement to my heart every day. I love you all so very much!

To the courageous friends who have shared their stories along the way and allowed me to share your experiences to help others—you've reminded me that there is a great need for this book, to be brave and give a voice to those of us in the shadows no matter what part you've experienced and to help others recognize there is more than the judgment from the world. There are people hurting and in need of the healing and hope found in Christ.

To my parents, thank you for laying the foundation for me as a child to know Jesus and understand that the Bible is true, trustworthy, and has the answer for everything we face in this life.

To the teachers, pastors, mentors, and friends who saw the true me and stood by me through my younger and adult years—I have never forgotten your grace and love!

ABOUT THE AUTHOR

Wife, mom to three, and bonus mom to four children, lover of music, athletics, good food, and outdoor activities, Laura Johnson does her best to love and impact the people God has placed in her life daily. Though her past holds great shame, it reminds her how much Christ has done to bring beauty from ashes. She simply wants to share this healing and hope in her every endeavor.

Originally from the East Coast, Laura grew up in a conservative Christian home and accepted Christ as her Savior at the age of four. She went on to attend Christian schools through elementary, high school, and college.

Laura graduated from Bible college with a Bachelor's in History Education and a minor in Biblical studies and later earned a Master's in Counseling to arm her as she carries out the mission Christ has given her.

Even after her rocky past, her passion from high school remains: she wants to love people and make an impact for Christ. Today, she celebrates her blessings in Michigan with her husband and their seven children and uses the lessons she learned from her indiscretions to minister to others who need hope and healing.

Connect with Laura at IAmTheOtherWomanBook.com

ARE YOU TIRED OF HIDING IN SHAME?

Discover a life where HE is the center and learn to create beauty from the ashes of your past.

KEYNOTE SPEAKER

START THE
CONVERSATION TODAY

TheHealingChapter1@gmail.com

CONNECT WITH LAURA

Hope and healing are possible from the impact of infidelity. Whether you are the "other person," the wounded spouse, a child of parental infidelity, a church, or community member, you can have hope and healing through Jesus.

@TheHealingChapter1   @LauraJohnson